A LEGACY

OF GRACE

On Maui

Our Story & Grace Bible Church, Maui

EDWARD S ASATO

A Resource of Exodus Book Publication

First Printing: September 2014

Cover: Jocelyn Alegre Asato

Published by Exodus Book Publishing
635 South Hina Avenue
Kahului, Hawaii 96732

ISBN 978-0-578-11992-2

Printed in the United States of America

Dedication

To *Susan Asato*, the best wife God could give a man, and to *Jonavan, Sharina and Davin*, our three children, their spouses and children who have done more for Jesus than we ever dreamt,

To the *early members* of Grace Bible Church Maui who believed in, supported and prayed for us,

To Jesus and you I give thanks for your love and faithfulness. Without you this book couldn't be written.

> *"You also helping together in prayer for us that thanks may be given by many persons on our behalf...."*   - 2 Corinthians 1:11

A Legacy of Grace

TABLE OF CONTENT

Dedication   3

Table of Content   5

Preface   7

Introduction   9

Chapter 1 – Discovering Jesus & His Church   11

Chapter 2 – Pioneering GBC, Maui   19

Chapter 3 – Building the House of God   27

Chapter 4 – Stewarding our Finances   39

Chapter 5 – Becoming A Blessing   45

Chapter 6 – The Legacy Continues   57

Appendix One – Susan's Story   61

Appendix Two – Eddie's Story   65

A Legacy of Grace

PREFACE

Pastor Eddie and Susan Asato founded Grace Bible Church Maui in September 1974. This book is a diary of their forty-year journey of faith.

Forty is a significant number in the Bible. A new earth was begun after it rained for 40 days in Noah's day. A new season of ministry was begun in Jesus' life after 40 days of temptation. A new realm - the Promised Land – was entered after 40 years of Israel's wilderness wandering. The number forty represents New Beginnings.

This book is not remembering the past for the sake of the past. It can be a compass for the uncharted waters of the future.

Before entering the Promised Land, the Israelites read and remembered the faithfulness of God for the previous forty years.

Israel's rehearsal of their past provided a *compass* as they moved into uncharted waters. Reviewing their history created *faith* for their future by remembering the power, mercy and faithfulness of God in the past. It also provided a sense of *identity*, because in reviewing their past, they saw God's unique call and destiny for their nation.

God made Grace Bible Church with a unique fingerprint that can be seen in the pages of this book. As I read this book, my faith was stirred for the future as well as a gratitude for the past.

My prayer is that it will do the same for you.

Jonavan Asato, Senior Pastor
Grace Bible Church, Maui

A Legacy of Grace

Introduction

"Then He said to them, 'Follow Me and I will make you fishers of men." — Matthew 4:19

Our story is about our call to follow Jesus and invite others to follow Him with us.

Susan and I responded to that call and began serving Him first at Grace Bible Church in Honolulu in its pioneer stages. During that time, God called many young people to pioneer churches across Hawaii and Asia.

God called us to begin one of those churches in Maui. Grace Bible Church Maui was part of the Spirit's momentum during a time God was spawning churches across Hawaii.

Through our life, we have asked *small* from God but God has always answered *big*.

A young lad offered a small gift to Jesus. Jesus used it to provide largely until thousands were fed with a surplus of 12 basketfuls. Jesus produced more than needed. John 6:1-13

When we began feeding a few families from our church facilities through Feed My Sheep, no one could dream then that all of Maui would have food provided for it. Jesus has literally taken little and multiplied it to feed multitudes today.

As a church, we almost purchased a 20,000 square feet property between two homes with no possibility for expansion. Architectural plans were designed and materials purchased. But the county government rejected our plans because God had other plans in mind. God wanted to provide more.

We couldn't imagine in beginning our preschool with the Montessori curriculum that we would develop the reputation of being one of the most highly recommended schools by families and grade school teachers without solicitation.

Because of the hardships we experienced, we never wished any of our children to engage in full-time church work. Our desire was for them to discover enjoyable career fields and served God in some local church. Never did we dream any of them desiring full-time church work. Not only do *some* of them desire full-time church work, *all of them* want to serve *with us on Maui.*

God uses and blesses us like that little lad with his bread and fishes providing for others as well as ourselves as we "seek first His kingdom and His righteousness."

"Now to Him who is able to do exceedingly abundantly above all that we ask or think according to the power that works in us."
- Ephesians 3:20

Chapter One
Discovering Jesus & His Church

"He has made everything beautiful in its time. Also He has put eternity in their hearts...."   - Ecclesiastes 3:11

A Quest for God

God has placed a sense of eternity in all of our hearts. Every person asks this question: "What Happens After Death?"

Did you ever pray this childhood prayer?

"Now I lay me down to sleep,
I pray the Lord my soul to keep.
And if I die before I wake,
I pray the Lord my soul to take."

My mother was taught that prayer by a neighbor and taught it to my brother and me. We'd kneel down by our bed each night to pray that prayer.

After two weeks of praying, I stopped after, " ... And if I die before I wake ..." And I wondered, "What will happen to me if I do die and never wake up?"

Similar questions led me in a quest for God:

Who created the sparkling stars I see at night?
What happens after death when one leaves his body?
What is the purpose of life beyond the material?
How does a person receive forgiveness of sins?
How can a person find lasting inner peace?

Those questions bothered me until at 15 years old I was invited to church and discovered Jesus Christ and the Bible.

Discovering Jesus Christ

Through the invitation of a high school friend, *Roland Kawano*, I attended Makiki Christian Church in Honolulu. Through a Teen Retreat I invited Jesus Christ into my heart and found the answer to all the questions I asked about life. My life was so radically changed that I began telling everyone I knew about Jesus Christ and what He could do.

Though reluctant to speak in public at first, I found a passion to share God's love with all my high school classmates. Because of that passion, God opened the doors to address the entire Iolani High School student body in two chapel services in my senior year. A thousand students heard the simple message of Jesus' power to change a life. I know a few that came to faith in Jesus but I'm thankful that everyone had a seed planted in their heart.

> *"...and the Lord said to me, 'Behold, I have put my words in your mouth."* - Jeremiah 1:9b

Experiencing the Power of the Spirit

Through a trip to Okinawa in my senior year of high school and a native interpreter for American missionaries, *Shinyu Kuniyoshi* , I was exposed to the Holy Spirit accompanied with speaking in tongues. I became hungry for the Spirit and searched for someone to teach me when I returned to Hawaii.

God sent Pastor *Hong Sit* of a Houston, Texas Baptist Church and Pastor *Harold Bredesen* from a Reformed Church in New York to Hawaii to teach about and pray for people for the infilling of the Spirit. 200 believers in the First Chinese Church in Honolulu were filled through Pastor Hong. About 30 college students received the Spirit and spoke in tongues through Pastor Harold Bredesen's workshop with the Inter-Varsity Christian Fellowship at the music department's Orvis Auditorium.

These teachings clarified Bible passages on the subject and convinced me that it was a major benefit for all believers. In the privacy of my home, I was filled and spoke in tongues.

What I didn't realize then was that I was being thrust into a global phenomenon sweeping the denominational and Catholic churches in the 60s and 70s called "The Charismatic Renewal."

"And do not be drunk with wine, in which is dissipation; but be filled with the Spirit."   - Ephesians 5:18

Through Harold Bredesen's contacts, God placed a key person in my life to help direct my future. He was a young pastor that Harold brought to the night meetings. He was the pastor of a newly planted church in Kalihi Valley. The church's name was Grace Bible Church. The pastor's name was *Mel Amrine*.

Discovering Grace Bible Church

I was headed for Wheaton College to prepare for my ministry career at the end of the summer of 1964. But my plans totally changed over the summer months.

I walked into my first Grace Bible Church Sunday evening service in June 1964. Only twelve members were in attendance, yet somehow they captured my heart.

I had no idea of the amazing future God planned for this church at that time. But this church would radically change the destiny of my life, open the doors to a global movement and take me around the world to witness it.

The Bredesen's meeting left many of us filled with the Spirit hungry for more. Pastor Mel offered Thursday evening

Bible studies near the campus to teach us about the gifts of the Spirit, healing and miracles. He taught us that they were still for today's church. He also took me aside personally and shared stories of God's miracles both in his and other people's life. I was convinced that Jesus was the same yesterday, today and forever.

I learned about Waco, Texas' Grace Gospel Church's Bible School where Mel and Doris received their training. This church was sending full-time ministers and missionaries across the US and the world sharing Jesus and the power of the Holy Spirit.

God spoke to me through the Scriptures and confirmed His directions through several dreams to lay aside my plans to attend Wheaton College. The Lord was clearly leading me to prepare to serve in Grace Bible Church, Honolulu.

One unexpected surprise as I chose this path was to find a close friend *Elmer Inafuku*, a college friend whom I introduced to IVCF and also to life in the Spirit, making that same decision.

We became partners in preparation for ministry over the next two years. Eventually, he would go to Japan to fulfill his spiritual destiny as I returned to Hawaii.

> *"... 'The Lord, before whom I walk, will send His angel with you and prosper your way...'"*   - Genesis 24:40

Preparing for Ministry in Waco

I was in ministry preparation for two years in Texas.

I learned much from the Bible about the contemporary "Charismatic Renewal" and operation of the gifts of the Spirit and heard stories from Spirit-filled ministers of God's supernatural miracles occurring in their evangelistic meetings and church planting efforts. I also spent several weeks with missionaries in Mexico witnessing the fruit of spiritual gifts helping national churches as well as American mission churches being pioneered in various Mexican cities.

I heard reports about a healing revival that powerfully impacted Argentina in the mid-50s led by *Tommy Hicks*. That revival was held nightly for six months, utilizing Buenos Aires' 60,000 seating coliseum that attracted overflowing audiences and impacting millions. Ambulances from nearby hospitals were bringing the sick for healing and those who died were being raised from the dead. Jesus was visiting Argentina!

"...he who believes in me, the works that I do will he do also and greater works than these he will do ...." - John 14:12

I was taught from the Bible, heard stories from many seasoned ministers and personally experienced God's power in my own life. All of these things were preparing me to reach those of my generation on Oahu's college campuses.

I returned two years later to Honolulu and the church I left with twelve members had grown to an average attendance of 50 on a Sunday morning.

"Though your beginning was small, yet your latter end would increase abundantly."   - Job 8:7

Confirming His Word with Miraculous Signs

Immediately upon working with college students God confirmed His Word with a miraculous sign.

Ron Hirai a star music student in the UH music program had the two biting edges of his upper front teeth filled miraculously with gold. He became an instant evangelist and many students became part of our college ministry and the church.

Young people were getting saved, baptized in water and filled with the Holy Spirit with the evidence of speaking in tongues.

> *"And they went out and preached everywhere, the Lord working with them and confirming the word though the accompanying signs. Amen."* - Mark 16:20

Within a few months, Pastor *Mel Amrine* felt God's leading to begin another church plant on the West Coast and asked *Ken and Beverly Spoerhase* to assume the senior leadership of Grace Bible Church. Pastor Ken's visionary leadership led the church into the next period of its membership growth, church-planting expansion and property acquisition.

The church added *Sam and Nancy Webb* as assistant pastors and *Esther Inafuku* as women's teacher, counselor and choir director.

Grace Bible Church grew to three hundred over the next eight years with a third of the congregation from the college and high school campuses.

Excited new converts were conducting Bible studies on four different campuses. I was busy with six or seven studies each week on three different campuses and in our home.

Middle school students from Kauai led by *Pat Ono* attended our high school and college summer camp. They requested a similar church started on their island. We sent college teams to begin the church. In 1972, Kauai Bible Church was officially begun with *Loyd and Esther Watanabe* set in as their first pastors.

Other churches spontaneously were started in Hawaii on Oahu, Hilo and Molokai. Overseas churches were begun in Sapporo and Tokyo, Japan and on the island of Guam.

Many of the church planters were those reached through our college ministry. Many others were nurtured in the church and are today serving across Hawaii, in the US mainland and in Asian nations through the influence of our Grace Bible Churches in Hawaii.

Who could have imagined that with that small beginning such a major work of thrusting ministries to nations of the world would result? Only the work of God's grace could multiply the seed sown and make it fruitful.

"A little one shall become a thousand, and a small one a strong nation; I the Lord will hasten it in his time."   - Isaiah 60:22

A Legacy of Grace

Chapter Two
Pioneering Grace Bible Church, Maui

" I will build My church and the gates of hell shall not prevail against it."   - Matthew 16:18

Eight years into our college ministry in 1973, I was sitting in a newly built 2nd floor college office with plush green carpet and a full-length picture window overlooking the city of Honolulu.

It was comfortable and beautiful!

We had just relocated the church from the cramped Kalihi Valley quarters to a larger property in Alewa Heights.

It was gratifying for me to finally have an office to work out of instead of my home. I had a beautiful view of the city and relished it. One day as I sat in my office enjoying the view, I felt the Lord speaking to me:

"Would you be willing to give up this plush office and go wherever I ask you to go?" And He awaited my response.

I remember kneeling down on that green carpet, with a reluctant but willing heart, saying, "Yes, Lord, I'll go where you want me to go."

I didn't realize then that the Lord had Maui on His mind.

Several years before God sent a young girl *Susan Shimabukuro* that swept me off my feet with her angelic glow and we were married on January 1974. She grew up on Maui and had a burden to begin a church there.

The Beginning

So starting a church on Maui initially was really Susan's idea, not mine. But God changed my heart by what He was about to do on the island.

God opened the hearts of a group of Catholic Charismatic women hungry for more of the Spirit. *Clytie Nishihara,* Susan's cousin appealed on behalf of this group. So, every

Wednesday, I would fly over to conduct a morning and evening Bible study. GBC Honolulu paid for all these church-planting expenses.

A faithful group of about fifteen individuals had come to faith in Christ through those weekly studies. God answered prayers and revealed Himself through some amazing miracles to confirm the word taught.

Confirming His Word with Signs Following

Over the years in our Maui church, we have seen God's mighty power to heal sicknesses and diseases. *Dianne Tamanaha* was healed of a bone cancer that her nursing profession friends deemed incurable. *Billy Martin* was healed of an incurable case of blood poisoning from a ruptured appendix. The MMH doctors gave him up to die. He was the only man with his condition ever to walk out alive. The doctors and nurses call him "The Miracle Man." *Lee and Doreen Yamashita's grandchild, Taesha,* was instantly healed of a severe chronic asthmatic condition. In one Easter service, beginning with *Lee Yamashita's* short leg, a dozen other short limbs were visibly lengthened before the entire church.

A book of healing miracles could be written of all whom God healed in miraculous ways like this.

But healing miracles accompanied God's Word even before our church was officially organized. This happened on one of our first trips to Maui.

"And they went out and preached everywhere, the Lord working with them and confirming the word though the accompanying signs." - Mark 16:20

Linda Craft of the Craft's Drug Store was on crutches due to a skiing accident. Her broken bones were supposed to heal after a month. Six months later she was still on crutches.

That's when she appeared in one of our first Wednesday evening Bible Study on Maui and received Jesus.

That night, we prayed for her bones to heal. The very next morning she got up without the use of crutches and made breakfast for her family for the first time in six months. God was validating His Word and Jesus' presence in Linda's life.

After a year, the group asked for an official Sunday church service to begin. Each week after returning from Maui, I believed that God would call another person to pastor the Maui church, not me.

But as I spent time with God in prayer, God reminded me of my commitment to trade my new office to go where He would lead. I clearly felt that He was speaking and leading us to Maui.

So, we officially began our services on September 1974 in the classrooms of Iao Intermediate School with Susan on a simple keyboard and myself on my guitar.

I was 30, Susan 26 and Jonavan was 10 months old.

Volunteers From Our College Ministry

Debbie Kim Jackson and *Dianne Tamanaha* were the fruit of our Oahu Grace Bible College ministry. Debbie had just graduated with an education degree and Dianne with a nursing degree. Both had a burden for Maui and a desire to support Susan and myself and the vision God had given to us for our Maui church.

They lived with us and became aunties to our children *Jonavan* and to *Sharina* and *Davin*.

The Lord Added to the Church

Within the first year, we began a week of healing and evangelistic services with *William Hartley* from England. He was one of the evangelists I had met in Waco, Texas in my two years of training. God used him powerfully in the gift of healing.

Many were miraculously healed in those services and families were added as well as single people.

Toshimi and *Katherine Higa* became part of our church as a result of those meetings. They were faithful members in our church through the years. Both have recently been taken to be with the Lord. Toshimi was a weekly worker in maintaining the church landscape pulling weeds and keeping the grass trimmed.

Over fifty persons came to faith in Christ as the healing power of Jesus was in display.

During this time our Honolulu church committed to support us for two years at $250 a month, but we were able to stand on our own financially within the first year.

Shortly after that, *Kevin Nishihara* came into our church as a single young man and joined one of the community households. He has been one of our faithful leaders and teachers over the years. He has served on our church board and helped lead our church's workshops and seminars. He and his wife, *June,* now work with Pastor Lance Sokugawa in our Wailuku Extension Church. Kevin is serving today as WEX's Director of Operations.

Christian Community and Church School

In the early years of our church life, we adopted a lifestyle of Charismatic Community "Households." We followed the Biblical example of Acts 2:44.

> *"Now all who believed were together, and had all things in common."* - Acts 2:44

We desired to launch a one room Christian school ranging from the elementary to high school ages. Debbie with her education degree was the perfect person to accept the challenge to set up the entire school.

And we had people like Dianne in the nursing profession and others in our household that contributed their entire paychecks that supported teachers like Debbie in our school who were not getting adequate pay from a start-up school.

MF and *Linnie Jackson* with their four children came from GBC Honolulu to work full-time as the principal of our Christian school. *Leroy* and *Lillian Wadahara* also came from our GBC Honolulu church to help us in the school and in our youth ministry. Everyone who worked in church and school were part of our Charismatic Community Households.

At one point we had 45 people in six different community homes contributing their entire paychecks in support of individuals working in different capacities in both the church and school. Both Susan and I with our three children also had a household of a total of 18 members for a year. This was an effective way to launch our church in its early stages.

Gay Wetter as a single parent with her five boys joined our church, attended our Christian school and was part of one of our community households. Her boys were mentored by some of the older men in the household. Gay was an assistant teacher in our school, worked as a nurse, is now retired and helps Feed My Sheep weekly. She is one of the early members in our church from our beginning history.

Weekly Women's Bible Studies

Ruth Kesaji, a woman with an evangelical background, contracted cancer and heard about God's power to heal. She participated in the Good Shepherd Episcopal Church's mid-week healing service. Good Shepherd's pastor *Richard Winkler* at that time was one of the Episcopal denomination's early charismatic leaders. Through God's grace and provision, Ruth was healed of cancer and served many in the ministry of healing.

Ruth wanted more Bible teachings to strengthen her faith and found out about our church. She asked for a weekday study to increase her knowledge of the Bible. So we set up weekly studies with her and the women she was helping through their difficult times for several years. She was a mother of faith to many of these young women.

Eventually, Ruth brought her husband *Cassius* and the women she spiritually cared for into our church and were faithful as members till the Lord took Ruth and Cassius home to be with him. Cassius was on our church leadership board for many years. Both served others in a ministry of healing until their death.

Ruth brought *Sandi Gomes and Lynn Iwamasa* to Christ, into our Bible Studies and then into our church as members.

Sandi has an amazing testimony of being delivered from depression and fear. She helped lead her husband Terry to Christ. As a member of our church, she has helped us with our music team, led the Cleansing Stream ministries and today is the lead intercessor in our WEX church today. She and Terry have volunteered the service of their trucking company for different needs of our church and have also helped other Maui churches.

Today, Sandi's daughter *Tami Patao* and Tami's husband *Dane Sr* are leaders in our WEX church. Dane and Tami's son *Dane Jr* is the worship leader for WEX and Dane Jr's wife *Sammy* works in our GBC preschool.

Lynn brought her husband *Thomas* to the church and into a relationship with Jesus Christ. Lynn worked in our office as a bookkeeper for many years and Tom volunteered his talent from his painting business to paint the two-story hall. He also painted the sanctuary interior walls and parking stall lines when it was built over ten years ago.

Both Sandi and Lynn were early members of our church.

The Crisis of the 80s

The 80s were filled with diverse challenges in our GBC churches and among the pastors. Many of our GBC churches faced crisis situations at the same time. We were facing our own in our Maui church that pressed us closer to the Lord.

We had adopted a church lifestyle that separated us from our Honolulu church and GBC family. But God eventually revealed to us that we were spiritual orphans and needed to restore our church family relationships. Our restoration was evidenced by the change of our name from Emmanuel Bible Fellowship to Grace Bible Church Maui.

During those years, Susan and I forged a close bond of friendship with *Sam and Nancy Webb* who since has become our closest ministry friends. Without their encouragement at different crucial crossroads, we would not have had the longevity in ministry we've experienced.

Both Pastor *Sam Webb* that took the senior pastor's role in our Honolulu church after Ken Spoerhase's tenure and myself as older pastors among younger took the leadership of our Grace Bible Churches and begun a tight knit monthly fellowship of all of our pastors. Grace Bible Ministries International was created.

As pastors we realized we needed each other to be successful. Strength and camaraderie among our family of pastors resulted. We worked together to assist our churches in the mission field as well as assist one another in our local ministries. We had annual conferences together and preached for one another's churches.

The crisis of the 80s was tough but it resulted in stronger churches, stronger relationships among pastors and more fruitful ministries for each of our churches.

A Legacy of Grace

Chapter Three
Building the House of God

When we came to Maui, I didn't want to purchase property or build buildings because we had just come from a major building project in Oahu using volunteer laborers that took years to complete. It was time-consuming, exhausting and it distracted from ministry.

I didn't want to engage in that level of distraction and we didn't ... for the first five years. But then God spoke.

And God spoke clearly enough to change my mind.

And His words were strong as they were clear:

"The people of Maui will not see permanence and stability without purchasing property and building facilities. Property and facilities will give you a lasting legacy that people will give their time, energy and finances to follow."

These words were shaking the convictions I had when I first came to Maui, but what else could I do if God was speaking?

"Let them make Me a sanctuary that I may dwell among them."
- Exodus 25:8

When God spoke those words to me, it was also accompanied with a surge of faith for finances. God also said, "I'm giving you $500,000. Act like you have it." And through the entire process, I felt I actually had that amount. Every day, I felt I was carrying $500,000 in the back pocket of my trousers.

A Nomadic Church

We rented our first office space on the 2nd floor of the Duco building at the corner of Lower Main and Mill Street. That gave me a place for prayer and study to prepare for our services and Bible studies.

We began our Sunday services at the Iao Intermediate School classrooms. At that same time, we utilized the Wailuku Union Church for our offices and our ACE Christian School classrooms. Later while our building was under construction, we rented the Kahului First Assembly of God Church facilities for our ACE Christian School and the Kahului Seventh Day Adventist Church for our Sunday services since they used their facilities on Saturdays.

We also rented Ala Lani Methodist Church, Salvation Army and Baldwin High School for some of our weekend worship services and weeknight Bible studies.

We had no permanent property and building and utilized eight different locations over the early six years.

This nomadic wandering confirmed God's word that families will not be drawn to God's kingdom without a sense of permanence. So we were in search for property to purchase.

While searching for property, I felt the Lord prompting us to rent a semi-permanent location that could be used through the week for Bible studies, worship services and accessible to the church 24 hours a day for prayer.

We found the location at the Puuone Business Plaza on Lower Main Street above Tokyo Tei and rented two office spaces.

Bob and Kathie Mundy with their sons, *Wesley and Jason*, became a part of our church during this time. Kathie assisted us in teaching our ACE school, currently leads our hula halau team and is a committed intercessor for our church. She and Bob also purchased one of the four homes we built and sold to pay off our first mortgage. They are part of our early membership prior to the acquisition of land and constructing buildings.

Other members from those early years are *Judy Taomoto* who regularly assists in our Sunday morning refreshment ministry and *Claire Ozai* who still attends our morning services when she is able.

It is upon faithful lives like these that the foundation of the early formative years of the church was established.

In Search of Permanence

Our church board, *Jim Lee, Cassius Kesaji, Robert Shimabukuro* and myself approached A&B to inquire of any available land for purchase.

A&B's property manager presented us with a property next to Lihikai Elementary School in the middle of a residential development. It was a two-house lot 20,000 square feet in size. Homes were already constructed on either side of the property that meant we would have no room for future expansion.

But our church was small in number and we could grow several times the size we were then. Plus we were excited about the prospect of ownership and development.

Russell Ito was one of our college students from Honolulu that had gone into the field of architecture. We employed his help. *Rick and Rose Shaw*, early pillars in our Kauai church, had a Lindell Homes franchise in Kauai and provided us with two two-story cedar homes at cost that could be used for our parsonages. God provided the right people at the right time.

Everything was set to purchase and develop the property.

And then, without warning, everything fell apart.

Disappointments and Delays

I remember the day clearly. I saw someone climbing the stairway to my office at Wailuku Union Church. It was the property manager from A&B. Normally he would call for a meeting at his office or notify us before he'd come. Because he didn't, I felt it was bad news. He walked over from the mayor's office located one block away and first apologized for the news he came to deliver.

It turned out that the mayor was against the sale of those lots to a church. For some reason, those lots were very special to him. He wanted it for workers coming from the Philippines contracted to work on the sugar plantations. And the mayor's plans held precedence over A&B and the church.

So, all deals were off the table.

But, as disappointing as this was, it was God's hand.

We didn't know then that this was God's way of protecting us from a bad decision. Later we would realize why.

"The king's heart is in the hand of the Lord, like the rivers of water; He turns it wherever He wishes." - Proverbs 21:1

I'm glad God often protects us from unwise decisions.

But there were times God chose not to protect us and allowed us to make unwise decisions that led to major disappointments but taught us vital lessons. Fortunately, this was not one.

Returning to our Family

At this time God was also dealing with us about restoring our family relationship with Grace Bible Church Honolulu. (See the previous chapter) And with that restoration of relationship came the following unexpected blessing.

God Raises Up A Cyrus

The news of the withdrawal of the contract to purchase land produced a deep disappointment in our church. But God sent a prophet from New Zealand, *Shaun Kearney*, to give us a word of faith to encourage us.

"Surely the Lord God does nothing, unless He reveals His secrets to His servants the prophets." - Amos 3:7

The following is a summary of the prophetic word:

"God will work behind the scene and move in the top levels of city government and raise up a Cyrus (the Persian king who released Judah to return to their land) who will assist you in acquiring the property you need. God will give to you more than what you were promised in the past. Believe and be encouraged in the Lord!"

God was revealing that He was at work behind the scene.

The A&B Manager felt so bad about retracting the contract that he was doing all he could to find land suitable for our needs.

Then, without warning or explanation, the mayor who stopped the sale resigned mid-term. A special election thrust an A&B executive and lobbyist into the mayor's office. God was working to promote a Cyrus who would not oppose our plans. Now both the new mayor and the A&B manager were acquainted with land purchase procedures and could agree on a suitable property for us.

In short time, a two-acre undeveloped parcel, which was four times the size previously offered us, was identified and presented to us for purchase. God was giving us something far better than we had settled for. A&B also paid for the infrastructure of water, electrical, curbing and roadway. The land was ready for the buildings we wanted to construct.

A&B also explained that there was an adjacent eight-acre parcel that they would develop into residential lots in the future that, once begun, would raise the value of our property. That was great news.

We were pleased at how God was working not imagining how much more He wanted to provide. We would later discover the wisdom and sovereign plan of God that would provide far more than what we envisioned in our Phase I development.

And we embarked on the first phase of our development.

Phase I: Homes and Building

Volunteers such as *Kevin Nishihara* and *John McCandless* from within our small congregation of less than a hundred members and willing workers from Oahu such as *Phillip Wong, Shoyei Tengan, Norman Dela Santos, Pat Mizut, John Murray* and *Mike Komatsu* dedicated their energies and talents to build four homes and a two-story building which was to be our church home until we would build our sanctuary.

Russell Ito redesigned the two two-story Lindell Homes to create four one-story homes on one acre. He also designed our simple two-story educational and office building that became our Sunday Worship location for over a decade.

Norman Fukumitsu, Susan's brother-in-law and former foreman for our Honolulu Grace Bible Church's major building project, was the only paid worker that coordinated the labor of dozens of people that daily volunteered to build.

Jim Lee, one of our early board members, volunteered two years of his time to work full-time with Norman to complete the project in slightly over two years. We owe a debt of gratitude to Norman, Jim and the scores of unnamed volunteers that helped make the project a success.

Jim and his wife *Brenda* always opened their home for holidays for the church, worked with our children's ministry and through their music business, Lee's Music Center, donated a consol organ, drums, sound equipment and the grand piano seen today on our church platform.

We eventually sold the homes to pay the debt owed to A&B. After the financial dust settled and accounting records tabulated, we had expended $500,000 and were debt-free. This was exactly what God promised me. God's promise became a reality!

Our plans were to build a 120 seating sanctuary immediately, but the exhaustion of over two years of constant building took its toll on all who volunteered daily for its construction. It would not be till over a decade later that we would actually build our sanctuary. But, as the disappointment, the delay proved to be a blessing.

At that time, we were not positioned to continue to build. The artisans we needed were not yet in our church, our finances were not replenished, our sanctuary design not settled and our faith needed to be further strengthened. Once these elements came together, we moved to Phase II!

Phase II: Building our Sanctuary

During the time we utilized our two-story sanctuary-office complex, the Lord taught us many significant lessons in developing a healthy congregation.

1) We discerned a judgmental and self-righteous attitude in our church and focused on Jesus' acceptance, forgiveness and love for the next two years,
2) We learned how to teach the Bible more clearly with a greater emphasis on the practical life of the believer,
3) We learned how to deal with chronic habits and sins in believer's life and provided annual Cleansing Stream seminars to deal with major issues everyone faces,
4) We learned and taught financial principles along with the tithe that prospered our church members financially as well as the church's bottom line, (See Chapter Four)
5) We took the gospel outside the church walls to bring the gospel to Maui's educational, business and political world, (See Chapter Five)
6) We also took steps to unite pastors and churches to reach the island of Maui together through prayer and outreaches in the marketplace, (See Chapter Five)
7) We linked our church with other Grace Bible Churches in a monthly supportive fellowship called Grace Bible Ministries International (GBMI) that eventually led us into our Every Nation global family.

At the same time we were learning lessons to grow a healthy congregation, God was adding to the church gifted people with significant construction skills to prepare us for the building of our sanctuary. Our congregation grew so we needed to conduct two Sunday morning services.

"Consider now, for the Lord has chosen you to build a house for the sanctuary; be strong and do it." - I Chronicles 28:10

We joined our two services into one service by renting out the cafeteria at Maui Waena Middle School. During this time, new architectural plans were designed for our sanctuary.

During the pre-2000 economic downturn, the blueprints were sent out for bid to different companies. The larger companies projected a cost of $1.3 million for our sanctuary. The *Betsill Brothers Company* currently headed by *Dwayne Betsill* is a Christian based company that came in at $950,000. They deducted their ten percent profit and did our project solely at cost.

We were able to further reduce that amount as skilled workers in our congregation did the electrical, plumbing, painting, stucco work and volunteered their time. Over $200,000 of expenses was saved. We ended the project having expended $750,000 nowhere near the over $1 million originally projected.

A few years before, God sent a wise and hardworking staff person to help us organize fundraisers, counsel women and lead women's Bible Studies. *Jean Oyama* was excellent in all these things, but she also became the project manager of our sanctuary construction. She did an amazing job handling the load of the day-to-day oversight and decision-making associated with building a church facility. She was the right person sent at the right time for the right task. She would later lead the launch of our church's preschool ministry. But that is for another chapter.

God also sent in major construction workers into our church during this time. One of the key men was *Tommy Lau Hee* who was the head of the Electrical Union on Maui. Because of the lack of jobs for electricians during our economic downturn, he enlisted the help of many of the men whose employment he supervised for our project. Volunteers completed the entire electrical work because of the Lord sending Tommy Lau Hee to our church at the right time.

Anthony Ventura, his sons *Brian* and *Dennis* and *Tom Kanaha* helped us with our stage, audio and visual control center, sound monitors and the cross on the sanctuary roof. *Adrian Iwamoto* designed our landscaping and *David Oyama* designed our stage.

Time and space does not allow the names of many other volunteers from our church and outside the church that assisted us to complete the construction of our new sanctuary and those who have helped to maintain our facilities and landscape.

The Unexpected Blessing

God works to clarify His will through sovereign connections independent of our initiatives.

> *"Trust in the Lord with all your heart and lean not on your own understanding; in all your ways acknowledge Him and He shall direct your paths."*   - Proverbs 3:5,6

As we were ending our sanctuary project, I received an unexpected call from a former church member. He called to inform me that his father intended to purchase the eight-acre parcel next to our property. His father was going to approach A&B about his proposal the next day. After the purchase of the property, they were willing to sell us one or two acres of the land. The call was to inform me of their intentions.

What the caller didn't know was that I was already negotiating with A&B for the purchase of those eight acres. I had an official letter in hand.

Let me explain how that happened.

A&B had not developed the adjacent eight acres like they projected. Over a decade had gone by. We were in need of some acreage to expand our operations.

A few months before that call, I had gathered a small group of intercessors to pray about the purchase of a portion of the eight acres. I presented my plans – the request to purchase two or three acres. The intercessors in unison felt from the Lord that I should request the purchase of the entire eight acres, not only a portion of it. I sensed they were right. My faith was too small and they were hearing from God.

I wrote the letter of request to purchase the entire eight acres and waited.

It was a Saturday night at about 10 pm. I wanted to retire early to be well rested for the following full Sunday schedule.

But I had an unopened stack of mail from the day on the lamp stand next to my bed. As I was opening the letters I noticed a letter from A&B. Anxious over their response, I opened the envelope. That letter robbed me of my sleep for the next hour.

As I read A&B's letter, I discovered what I thought was a secretarial mistype. It stated they were willing to sell the eight-acre parcel for $400,000 - I couldn't believe my eyes! I thought the secretary mistyped one zero and the sum should have read $4,000,000. To buy a residential zoned 8-acre property for $400,000 was unthinkable.

But even with this amazing opportunity, I still struggled with committing our church to a greater financial burden than we had assumed with the cost of our sanctuary. So, I hesitated to respond for a week. God knowing my hesitancy moved on our former church member to call. Receiving that call alerted me that we could lose the property if we didn't make a decision quickly.

The next day I called for an appointment and took a few of our board members to secure the transaction, hoping that A&B hadn't received the other offer. But the other offer was already in their hands. As people of integrity they honored their word to us in spite of a higher offer.

And they went further. They settled for $50,000 less than what they originally asked.

We were now close to completing our new sanctuary. And at the same time we were proud owners of a large eight-acre zoned Residential III property adjacent to our two acres with a price tag of $350,000. Unbelievable!

We were positioned not only to minister to more people in our sanctuary. We were also well positioned into the next few decades of growth and opportunity with our new acquisition.

"And we know that all things work together for good to those who love God, to those who are the called according to His purpose."
                                                            - Romans 8:28

A Legacy of Grace

Chapter Four
Stewarding Our Finances

"Beloved, I pray that you may prosper in all things and be in health, just as your soul prospers."   - III John 1:5

We have heard many testimonies of God's financial blessings on our church members over the years as a result of their commitment to tithing.

One couple that struggled with giving their tithe was pleasantly surprised at the results once they wrote their first tithe check.

When the husband went to work on the Monday after they tithed he found the company he worked for had raised his pay to the exact amount they committed to tithe monthly.

Their tithe released the increase of their income. They gave God their tithe and didn't have less to spend.

This was their testimony: "If we knew how God would bless our finances as we tithed, we would have tithed earlier."

This same testimony is duplicated over and over again. I could fill many pages with these testimonies. We have many of our own personal stories to share as well.

As important it is to understand the tithe, it is equally important to understand the whole arena of financial stewardship: making, budgeting, spending, saving, investing and giving money. Giving the tithe is one of seven aspects of financial stewardship.

But like many pastors teaching on the subject of finances I only focused on the tithe as we began.

Teaching the Church to Tithe

Susan and I had been tithing for two decades and saw how God blessed our finances beyond what we expected. We gave without expectation of return and became living proof that God blesses those that tithe. Though God blessed us, I didn't feel it appropriate to teach our church about tithing.

One of the reasons I hesitated teaching on tithing was that I didn't want to be misunderstood as having ulterior motives in asking people to give.

The second reason I didn't teach tithing was that I didn't want guests and visitors to think the church was only after their money.

But in spite of those objections, God dealt seriously with me about teaching the tithe. God's desired that His people would be blessed and it could only fully happened if they understood giving.

He asked me: "How can you expect members to be blessed in their finances if they never learn to tithe? Tithing was necessary for their benefit, not the church's."

The Lord's rebuke was Biblical so I began an annual systematic teaching on tithing to the church.

As a result, different families and individuals began seeing God's blessings on their income and the income of their businesses. They were learning as we did that there was a blessing in giving.

So, even though our church's income increased it didn't solve the problem of our church's monthly deficit. We still had more bills at the end of a month. I had yet another lesson to learn that involved more than the tithe.

Seeing a Bigger Financial Picture

God personally dealt with me about caring for my family's financial future – Susan and my retirement income, our children's college fund and saving for large purchases.

God spoke to me from I Timothy 5:8, "If anyone does not provide for his own … he has denied the faith and is worse than an infidel."

Through God's personal rebuke and my response to discipline my financial stewardship for my family's sake, I began to learn and implement plans for budgeting, savings, investments and insurances.

Through that experience I also became aware of the church member's need to wisely steward their assets.

Out of it grew annual Sunday sermon series on the general stewardship of money and weekend seminars on a gamut of subjects from buying homes, borrowing monies, investing monies and the value of insurance products.

Through this balanced presentation of finances to our church, the church became healthy in their personal financial disciplines that resulted in greater blessings in their lives. And for the first time, our church budget had surplus cash.

But God had one more lesson to teach us in the arena of finances.

Finances and Our Every Nation Family

Interestingly enough, our next lesson with finances was connected to our search for and becoming part of a global church family, Every Nation Churches and Ministries.

Our Grace Bible Church family in Hawaii was limited in its network of contacts in the foreign mission fields so we were looking for a global family to belong to.

Sam and Nancy Webb from our Honolulu church was spearheading that search. They researched almost a dozen groups. But none seem to fit us. Our search narrowed to seriously consider the Every Nation Church and Ministries. So we met their leaders and went to many of their major annual conferences to evaluate the match.

I had just returned from an Asia ministry trip in 2001 and the topic of global ministry was on my mind. Young people in our church, and especially my daughter *Sharina*, were seeking ministry opportunities in Europe and Africa but we had no connections in those regions. Asia was our primary focus of ministry. We needed to enlarge our scope. We needed a larger family.

Susan and I were in Anaheim, California, for a global Every Nation conference. Through that conference, God spoke to us to join this family of churches. We were also encouraged to pray through the week about what we could give financially on the final day of the conference. So, Susan and I prayed about the amount to give.

The final day arrived. Susan and I wrote on separate pieces of paper what God laid on our hearts. We traded sheets. She looked at mine and I looked at hers. God had spoken similarly to both of us and we were pleasantly surprised.

We both wrote the figure - $5,000! But that was $5,000 we knew we didn't have in our checking or savings accounts. This was the first time God asked us to give funds we didn't have. We were trusting God for the provision.

We didn't realize then that the provision was already on route to us. God was going to use Pastor *Rich Marshall*, a contact from *Ed Silvoso's* Harvest Evangelism, as a key person to release finances for our church and us. (More on Ed Silvoso in Chapter Five)

Rich was scheduled to speak on the subject of marketplace ministry the Sunday we arrived back on Maui. When he arrived at our service, he greeted me and asked if he could change his message. He felt the Spirit asking him to speak on finances. I didn't give it a second thought and consented. That was the first time I heard a message on the "Firstfruits Offering."

Firstfruits Giving I never knew that the "Firstfruits Offering" was a separate offering from the tithe.

I knew about the tithe and began tithing to the Lord after I was taught that it was Biblical. And then God challenged me to regularly teach our people to tithe. But I had never heard about the "Firstfruits Offering."

The Firstfruits Offering represented the *entire increase* of a regular monthly income to be totally given to the Lord in the first month and then tithed on from the second month. If your income increases by $500 a month, $500 is given to the Lord in the first month and then a tithe of $50 a month given from the second month on.

It was also to be given to the Senior Leader of the church.

At the end of his message, Rich asked people to bring their firstfruits to the front. People brought the increase they had experienced over the past few months. That Sunday, it totaled $5,000, exactly what we committed to give to Every Nation. But before the week was over, another $5,000 was given. By the end of the year a total of $40,000 was given as a Firstfruits Offering. That represented a total amount of income increase of close to $500,000 for all members in our congregation together.

The week after the initial offering, I asked our bookkeeper to not cash the checks until I studied the Bible to verify the teaching we were given. After a week of study, I found the Bible documenting all that Rich taught us that Sunday.

By that divine appointment with Rich Marshall, God allowed us to fulfill our financial commitment to Every Nation. But at the same time He began to open a doorway to financial blessing that added $500,000 to the overall annual income of our church families that year.

Our giving to Every Nation opened a floodgate of financial releases we could not have imagined could happen.

God was confirming our faith in giving, teaching us about a unique Firstfruits Offering and verifying our step to belong to a global family, Every Nation.

Offerings Blesses the Church and the Givers

Along with the tithe and Firstfruits Offering, we encourage our church to give general offerings for special causes such as Feed My Sheep, youth mission teams, special guest speakers, emergency needs and building project funds.

When September 11th happened and the Twin Towers collapsed, many churches faced financial hardships and trimmed their budgets. That didn't happen to us. I believe it's because of the "Offering."

Feed My Sheep Our feeding program was already underway. God promises in His word to preserve those who help the poor with their offering. As a church, we committed over $1,000 a month to FMS.

> *"He who has a generous eye will be blessed, for he gives his bread to the poor."* — Proverbs 22:9

New York Church Plant As result of 9/11, our Every Nation family decided to help rebuild New York by beginning a new church to encourage the city. Our board members agreed to give one total Sunday morning offering which is one fourth of our monthly budget toward the church plant. What was given that Sunday was above our average Sunday offering, but we made our monthly budget even while giving away one week of income.

Purchasing Our 1st Property As already mentioned, we had the opportunity to purchase two acres of land. What I didn't explain was the need for a large down payment. The church at that time didn't have the amount needed.

So we collected what we could from our church members but that was not enough. So God spoke to Susan and me.

We had a nest egg of $12,000 from the sale of our Oahu condo to be used for a home purchase in Maui. One day while Susan and I were praying we both felt God ask us to give that total amount toward the needed down payment. That amount was the most sizeable offering given for that purpose and enabled the church with our small membership to purchase our first property.

Because of offerings like this from our church, we have been able to obey God's word to us to "buy property and build facilities" for a lasting legacy on Maui.

We feel like that young lad that brought his five loaves and two fishes and entrusted them into the hands of Jesus Christ. We gave of our lives and what we possessed. As a result, multitudes have been fed by the miraculous grace of Jesus Christ.

The next chapter on "Becoming A Blessing" explains what fruit has resulted on Maui from investing in God's kingdom in this way.

"Most assuredly, I say to you, unless a grain of wheat falls into the ground and dies, it remains alone; but if it dies, it produces much grain."   – John 12:24

Chapter Five
Becoming A Blessing

"...So I will save you, and you shall be a blessing; do fear not, let your hands be strong."   - Zechariah 8:13b

"If you closed the doors to your church, would your community miss you?"

That question bothered me because I couldn't say, "Yes, our community would miss us."

Yes, we worked with those who walked into our services, led them to Christ and helped them grow in their faith. But our vision did not go beyond those who came to us. Our vision didn't include a strategy to go out and change our community.

I was challenged to do something that would go beyond the four walls of our building and impact the community.

I first heard this question repeated at different Harvest Evangelism conferences hosted by its founder *Ed Silvoso*.

But Ed not only asked the questions, he also had answers gained from the birthing of movements of city transformation from around the world.

It was through his teachings and books on "Prayer Evangelism", "Anointed for Business", "That None Should Perish" and "Transformation" that our church began to reach outside its walls working with other Maui churches to change Maui's spiritual landscape.

This is part of our story.

Prayer Evangelism

Prayer Walking One person can change their community.

Susan Begley from Harvest Evangelism came to Maui and shared her testimony of prayer walking her neighborhood and seeing God transform the street she lived on.

Drug lords dominated her neighborhood and drug purchases brought undesirable activities and people to that community. The street wasn't safe so most people stayed indoors. But Susan and her husband took a bold step. They decided every day to walk their neighborhood and pray for each home. They invited God's presence to invade their community.

A few months later, the drug houses closed. A preschool opened in its place and new neighbors moved in. The neighborhood was changed because she and her husband prayed. That was something every Christian could do.

We began teaching prayer walking our communities to the members of our church. And many began implementing it immediately.

We started first by organizing teams that would prayer walk the community immediately around our church facilities.

"Every place that the sole of your foot will tread upon I have given you ...." – Joshua 1:3

We saw immediate responses to our prayer walking. New families from the neighborhood around us began attending our morning services. This was just before building our sanctuary and those being added were those with construction skills that would help us with the project of constructing our sanctuary. God was at work as we prayed.

As we prayed for God's blessings on our community, God began by blessing our church. This was the first tangible result of God answering our prayers.

GBC & Maui Prayer Ministry Prayer for our church, its leaders and pastors has been the key to see much of what God has done in reaching people for Christ, healing physical sicknesses, restoring relationships and releasing God's presence in our weekend services. There are many testimonies that could be written from lives that have been changed and families that have been restored. *Robin Ventura* has functioned as the lead intercessor in our church and has enlisted the support of many other women in this ministry. She currently works in this area in our church and also coordinates an island-wide prayer focus with key intercessors from many other Maui churches monthly.

Pastors United to Pray In 1996, 400 Christians gathered from dozens of Maui churches for a 3-Day conference to embrace a vision of changing the spiritual climate of Maui through prayer. *Ed Silvoso* the Founder of Harvest Evangelism shared that vision. The coordinator for that event was a woman who led an inter-church prayer ministry in Maui, *Joyce Kawakami*.

Ed's first step of implementation was for pastors to form weekly prayer meetings in different locations across Maui. Denominational differences faded as pastors gathered to pray together.

My two close pastor friends were from different church backgrounds – one was a Nazarene, *Dale Kreps*, and the other was a United Church pastor, *Vernon Tom*. We together led the pastors and churches in Maui in building a united pastor's fellowship. We worked and prayed together with pastors in weekly prayer meetings and a few annual prayer retreats.

> *"As they ministered to the Lord and fasted, the Holy Spirit said,*
> *'Now separate to Me Barnabas and Saul for the work to which*
> *I have called them."*   - Acts 13:2

We can validate that, as a result of those prayer times, at least two pastors were thrust into church planting ministries – Pastor *John DeMello* of the House of Restoration in Keanae, Hana and Kahului, and Pastor *Greg Dela Cruz* of Living Way Church in Wailuku. Their churches were the tangible outgrowth of those prayer efforts.

And many more other churches were planted across Maui and Hawaii over the years. Today all the public school facilities are rented by pioneer churches so that movie theaters, hotels and shopping centers are the only available locations to begin new churches.

As a result, Maui church attendance has gone from 10% of the population 20 years ago to 30%+ in 2014. Maui has seen tangible results from pastors united in prayer.

United Prayer Event Our church engaged in prayer efforts with other Maui churches. Pastor *Robb Finberg* from Grace Church led an all-night prayer event at Baldwin High's War Memorial Gymnasium. He initiated this event as a result of one of our annual Maui Pastor's retreat. Hundreds from many church traditions gathered to pray together for Maui. Before the next week was over, a stalled Maui economy was reinvigorated, a three-year drought broken and the largest drug bust in Maui's history took place. God answered the prayer of Maui's churches.

Marketplace Ministry

Marketplace Ministry. Business people learned that they were ministers of Christ. They were not second-class citizens of the church. They were as anointed in business as pastors for ministry in the church. Money was not evil. Money could be used to advance God's kingdom. All these thoughts were based on fresh Biblical insights. Consider these examples from the Bible.

Joseph, a government leader was the first person recorded in the Bible that the Spirit fell upon. Aholiab and Beezeleel were artisans for Moses' tabernacle and were anointed by the Spirit for their construction work. Jesus was a firstborn son that took his father's role as CEO of the family carpentry business before His spiritual ministry.

Ed Silvoso's book *Anointed For Business* explained the role of these Bible character and challenged ordinary people to be ministers of Jesus in their marketplace world.

The Bible taught that God's anointing was upon government and business leaders before it fell upon priests of the tabernacle and temple.

As our church understood their role as marketplace ministers in the business world they carried the influence of the church from the building into the marketplace. As our congregation began to understand this it changed their lives and their marketplace influence.

Kenny Ching, F&B manager of Royal Lahaina, faced a public relation campaign against the hotel that threatened its profitability. Understanding his role as a pastor and intercessor in his marketplace stopped the tide of that negative campaign, miraculously restored a washed out beachfront and brought profitability back to his hotel.

Myles Kawakami, president of a large carpet business in Maui, placed his business up for sale because of a projected large financial loss. When the Lord requested a 50% share of his business and he consented, a miraculous momentum shifted a year of predicted loss to years of multiplied profit. As a result, God used his business to help the poor and hungry on the island. His workplace became a platform for ministry to the needy. Today, many are part of the 51% Club inspired by his testimony.

Kathy Mannoia, president of a tax accounting service, was a frustrated Christian businesswoman that desired to be used in a greater way. She was inspired with a fresh vision to use her business as a platform for ministry. Today, her staff begins the day with prayer and offer prayer for their clients during the business day. As a result, salvation, healing and restoration of lives are taking place through her tax preparation firm. Her business has tripled in size and people call in their prayer requests to their office and staff as they would call a church to pray for them. God's kingdom is being released through her business.

There are dozens of stories similar to this from members of our church who have realized they are called into the marketplace as ministers of Jesus Christ.

Today, the church makes its impact through the week in the marketplace not only in our services on Sunday.

Helping the Poor and Hungry

"Is this not the fast that I have chosen ... is it not to share your bread with the hungry..."   - Isaiah 58:6,7

The Lord spoke from Isaiah 58 so clearly one day in a time of prayer and fasting in 2001: "Develop a ministry to feed those unable to buy food for themselves. Find someone in the church to oversee this ministry." It was so clear I began the search.

What I didn't realize that I was the answer to a prayer on the heart of one of the members of our church.

Feed My Sheep. When I prayed about the person to ask, God revealed *Joyce Kawakami* to me. I asked Joyce if she would organize a feeding program from our church facilities, tears flowed down her cheek. I didn't realize that from 1998 she was already feeding families, wanted to help more families and was praying for people to come alongside to help.

I thought Joyce was the answer to my prayer, but I was really the answer to her prayers.

So Joyce moved the ministry of feeding from the back of her car to one of the rooms in our church hall. People from our church and other churches pitched in to help.

Feed My Sheep was born.

The initial goal was to feed twenty families. But God had other plans.

Joyce received a vision from the Lord to provide a week of food for every person that requested help.

Pastor *Jonavan Asato* a few years later launched Stomp Out Hunger to fundraise to open more locations to cover all of Maui. $65,000 was raised to open the needed remaining locations all over Maui so food could be available to everyone on the island.

Today, there are five locations supplied by six staff personnel driving several trucks that provide thousands of meals weekly. Everyone on Maui has food available through these locations.

But not only do the needy receive food, every person is also offered prayer. There are many who have been saved, healed and spiritually ministered to on a weekly basis. There are weekly testimonies of God at work in the hearts of the hungry in body, soul and spirit. Feed My Sheep functions like a mobile feeding church with an island-wide membership.

Who could have imagined that Feed My Sheep would have that powerful a coverage to meet the physical and spiritual needs of an entire island?

Community Outreaches

GBC Preschool Our church administrator *Jean Oyama* had a vision of beginning a preschool to reach non-churched parents and children. She envisioned more than a babysitting program and found the Montessori curriculum as the best to train young children in preparation for kindergarten.

As we were ready to begin, our GBC Honolulu had just sold their property and closed down their preschool. All their material, furniture and resources were offered and shipped to us.

Janice Yahiku, Susan's cousin from Oahu had that Montessori background and came to Maui to train our teachers. She worked for GBC Honolulu's preschool but was now free to assist us. She worked with a great team of teachers and one of the teachers, *Kama Tempo*, already had a Montessori background.

The school was launched in 2006 and has had nothing but positive feedback from its outset. The parents from our school and elementary teachers from the community recommend the school without our solicitation. Some parents register their children several years in advance.

Several years ago, *Sharina Husted* worked with Jean to begin an annual church and preschool Sunday Christmas service. The preschool children have a large part of the service so many of their parents and family members are in attendance. Many parents have received Christ and have become part of our church today and many others have connected to Jesus Christ through other relationships.

Operation Christmas Child God placed on *Debbie Rodrigues'* heart a desire to reach children with the gospel in other nations. The avenue she found was through Good Samaritan founded by Franklin Graham, son of Billy Graham that gave Christmas gifts with a message of Jesus to children across the globe. Originally, she wanted to mobilize our church members to be involved. God had other plans.

Today she coordinates twenty-six Maui churches to reach the children of Nepal. For the Christmas of 2013, 3,271 Christmas boxes were shipped from Maui to Nepal. Through Debbie's leadership, our Maui churches are reaching thousands of Nepal's children with the gospel.

Wailuku Extension Church On Easter 2007, we sent out forty members to begin an extension church in the town of Wailuku. *Lance and Tedynne Sokugawa* was ordained as the lead pastor over the extension.

Lance came to Jesus as a teenager, grew up in our Grace Bible Church family in Honolulu, assisted in two church plants, Hilo Bible with *Roy and Helen Kim* and GBC West Oahu with *Sidney and Gail Sumida*. Tedynne grew up in Maui and became a Christian in Grace Honolulu. They both met in church, married and came to Maui in 1994.

They helped oversee our youth ministry for several years. But Lance had a call from God to pastor a church. With a full-time job managing a golf course, he couldn't see how that call could be fulfilled. Our Every Nation churches in Manila developed a model of one church functioning in different locations that helped us strategize how to release Lance to pastor while still working full-time.

Today, many new families, teens and children are being reached through our WEX church.

Other Outreaches Our daughter, *Sharina Husted* returned with her husband *Ryan* and four children to Maui in June 2010 to assist us as our executive administrator. She launched a successful Summer Sports Camp that reached two hundred children several years ago. She also coordinates an annual Trunk 'O Treat a safe Halloween alternative where car trunks of members are decorated and used to give out candies to neighborhood children and families in our church parking lot. That event attracts about a thousand people annually. The event includes games for children in our sanctuary, food under our porte-cochere and prayer offered to every person in a prayer tent. She also coordinates our monthly Ohana Sunday that addresses different aspect of family life and children's needs attracting new families to our church.

Youth Ministry in our church is led by Pastor *Jonavan Asato* and has reached hundreds of teens in many high schools on Maui over the past decade. His leadership impacted the Kamehameha and Baldwin High School campuses. In Kamaehameha, a large percentage of the senior class was in small group studies on campus and during that time our youth services hit an all time peak. He aligned his ministry with other youth pastors and churches to serve Maui's schools and communities with practical acts of kindness because of a vision of transforming our community. Jonavan was blessed to have the addition of two full-time youth staff for a few years: *Tyson* and *April Lum* on MPD support from Every Nation and *Matt Jackson* from our Guam Grace Bible Church.

Reaching Nations

From the beginning of our Grace Bible Church in Honolulu, we have always believed that every local church should support ministers on the foreign mission fields. We have committed 10% of our finances to support these missionaries and ministers in other nations of the world.

Not only have we financially supported many of those missionaries, we have also sent teams annually to encourage and strengthen them.

We also commit our finances for church planting and leadership development in our monthly support of our global Every Nation family.

Mission Teams In previous years, Pastor *Jonavan* has mobilized youth mission teams to the Philippines, China and Okinawa. Last year they went to Bali and this year to help our Kauai church. We can expect more teams to go out next year.

Financial Support Over the decades, we have regularly supported churches and missionaries in different fields.

We've adopted *Paul Sarchet-Waller*, a missionary from England in his church planting effort in Hong Kong and his outreaches to the Philippines, India and Burma.

Daniel Kikawa is a Grace Bible ordained minister in Hilo, Hawaii. He was the visionary for the "Io Project" over a decade ago that helped native Hawaiians restore their spiritual roots in faith in Jesus Christ. The Hawaiian Christian community has grown from under 10% decades ago to almost 50% today. He teaches unique cross-cultural insights that help missionaries more effectively reach the nations they are called to serve.

We have also supported other missionaries serving in mission fields over the years. They are missionaries in Japan - *Elmer & Yoshanne Inafuku* in Shinjuku, *Scott & Naomi Douma, Ted & Loren Kawabata* and *James & Karen Coble* in Yokohama, *Glen & Linda Nabarette* in Tokyo. We also support *Kaui & Jeannie Tai* in Bangkok and *Henry Romero* in Manila.

We also support the efforts of Harvest Evangelism and its founder Ed Silvoso regularly as they lead efforts to transform nations across the world. They are seeing great fruit in changing destitute nations to vibrant spiritual forces for God's kingdom especially in Asia and South America.

There are many more in our Hawaii family of pastors and missionaries that we pray for but don't regularly support with financial provisions.

Ministry & Teaching Outreaches Over the years, God has used Susan and myself to assist pastors in their church planting efforts in Sapporo, Tokyo, Yokohama and Shibuya, Japan. We've also have had the privilege to minister to churches in Malaysia, Philippines, Singapore, Hong Kong, Thailand and Sakhalin, Russia. Recently, we have held annual conferences for pastors, churches and leaders in Okinawa, Yokohama and Tokyo.

> *"blessing I will bless you and multiplying I will multiply your descendants ... and in your seed all the nations of the earth shall be blessed."*   - Genesis 22:17,18

A Legacy of Grace

Chapter Six
The Legacy Continues

History and Bible prophecy predicts a marvelous future for the church.

> *"But the path of the just is like the shining sun that shines ever brighter unto the perfect day."* - Proverbs 4:18

Our Maui story is only one small segment of Jesus' church in Hawaii and around the world. If our story were multiplied thousands of times we can see the reason why God's kingdom today is expanding at a phenomenal rate. And the church will continue to expand in an ever-increasing manner.

> *"Of the increase of His government and peace there will be no end …and over his kingdom … The zeal of the LORD of hosts will perform this."* - Isaiah 9:7

A marvelous legacy has been passed down to us from those who came as missionaries and church planters to Hawaii to deliver God's good news in Jesus Christ.

We have attempted to pass this legacy on to our churches and our families so that legacy can continue into future generations.

God's plan is one day to saturate every nation of the world with the good news of His love before Jesus Christ returns.

> *"And this gospel of the kingdom will be preached in all the world as a witness to all the nations and then the end shall come."*
> - Matthew 24:14

The next generation of pastors and missionaries from our churches and our families will be gifted with talents and passions greater than ours. They will do exploits far outpacing anything we have ever accomplished or even hoped to accomplish.

This is the bright future God promises for His church and our families. A transition of leadership to younger generations is taking place in His church on a global scale. And this promises an irreversibly bright future.

Jesus is building His church and giving us the privilege to cooperate with Him as He builds His church through our lives, our families and future generations.

"The glory of this latter temple shall be greater than the former, says the Lord of Hosts." - Haggai 2:9a

Appendices

A Legacy of Grace

Appendix One

Finding Jesus - Susan's Story

I graduated from Baldwin High School with aspirations of becoming the Best Band Teacher in Hawaii.

This was the result of my Band teacher, Mr. Saburo Watanabe, a man I deeply respected and loved. I was determined to be like Mr. Watanabe in every way, not just academically, but in his character. He talked to us for many hours about life, integrity and character but he never mentioned Jesus Christ in his talks. But I somehow knew that he was a strong Christian believer and if I was going to be like Mr. Watanabe, then that meant my becoming a Christian as well.

I made a decision to become a Christian sometime in my four- year journey at the University of Hawaii College of Education majoring in music.

One day all the music students were talking about Ron Hirai who was one of the top musicians in the department. Ron was quitting his music career to become a minister. I was curious to meet him, more because of his music abilities, since he seemed to be a "legend" in the music department.

Ron would come on campus regularly and invite me to Bible studies. Long story short, I started attending Grace Bible Church.

It was a two-year struggle at not understanding the Bible, it's language and doctrines (how do you explain words like justification, sanctification, consecration, or just "faith" to an unbeliever?) but I was experiencing God's presence for the first time in my life.

The struggle for my soul finally ended when I made a decision to go to Grace Bible's Youth camp instead of working at my summer job at the pineapple cannery in Maui to pay for my tuition. At the end of camp, I became a new person and lost the passion to become the best band director in the State of Hawaii. (I also forgot that I was addicted to cigarettes) I cancelled my plans to transfer to a University in Washington. I already had my dorm roommate's name. I only wanted to remain in Grace Bible Church and learn more about God in the powerful services that were happening at that time.

I started understanding the Bible for the first time and wept reading through the story of Joseph and his brothers. As I learned the precious Bible truths for the first time on Restoration, and seeing God's Plan throughout the Bible from Genesis to Revelation, experiencing worship services at Grace Bible Church, I started yearning for Maui to experience what I was experiencing and seeing how wonderful God was.

I shared my experience with many pastors on Maui, some asked me to teach in their services, others showed me the door. I invited teams to come with me to Maui, stay at my parent's home, fed them, used my parent's cars, (what else are parents for?) and we played music and prayed for people, shared our testimonies at hospitals, shopping centers, where ever we could.

At that time, ignorance (of proper protocols, procedures, permissions, etc) was bliss. I wanted to be the pastor of a church on Maui and dreamed of knocking on every door of every household on Maui, all by myself.

But God had other plans and He spoke very clearly to me that I needed a husband, and he would be the pastor of the church on Maui. Enter: Eddie Asato! God provided.

In September 1974, we started a church on Maui, sent by Grace Bible Church Honolulu with a typewriter and a promise of $250 per month for two years. If we couldn't be independent after two years, we could return to Honolulu and forget about Maui. [But God was gracious and we were self-supporting by the end of the first year.]

I have found people who are more in love with Maui than I am. Joyce Kawakami, before becoming a Christian in her 7th grade class fell in love with the map of Maui and decided she would move to Hawaii at graduation.

A Legacy of Grace

Appendix Two

How I Became A Christian – Eddie's Story

"Who Made the Stars?"

I was a freshman at the University of Hawaii and found myself sitting in the home of my aunt, who babysat me when I was young. I had scheduled a sales appointment with her to present my Zylstra China product line that helped put me through college while, at the same time, helping a close friend start his business.

My aunt asked me what I was planning to do after college. I told her I was seriously considering being a missionary to South America. Her response surprised me.

She said, "I always thought you would go into some field like that from the time you were a young child." Then she proceeded to relate an experience I had no conscious recollection of.

She said, "You were about 5 years old and I was taking care of you. It was nightfall. We walked in the back yard of my home and looked above us at the countless sparkling dots of lights peering through the dark sky. The night sky was beautiful!"

"Then you asked me a question that both startled and puzzled me. You asked, 'Who made those beautiful stars?' It startled me because you were so young and puzzled me because I had no answer."

"It was what you said next that made me realize there was something special about you. You said to me, 'One day I'm going to find out who created the stars!'

"That's why I'm not surprised that you want to be a minister for God."

"Where Do We Go After We Die?"

That question bothered me but I never asked my mom for an answer. And I remember asking that question again at my grandma's funeral.

My grandma's funeral was filled with an unpleasant odor of incense, dull chanting and a monotonous recitation. I wasn't comfortable with such a depressing atmosphere.

I moved forward with a young friend to the casket where my grandma lay still. I tried talking to her and asking her questions like I was used to but she gave no response or answer. She just lay still so unlike the lively woman I had known.

Immediately, something inside me told me she was gone. Her body was present but somehow the person inside was missing. I knew as a child I was viewing an empty corpse. She had gone somewhere I couldn't see or know. She was in another world. I didn't know where but somehow I knew I would one day find out.

The Invitation that Changed My Life

In November 1959, I found myself at the Kokokahi YMCA campgrounds in Kaneohe, Oahu. Our church's Christian Endeavor Group was holding its annual Thanksgiving Youth Camp.

I was there because of a simple invitation from Roland Kawano, a fellow classmate at Iolani High School. He invited me to join him one Sunday at his church. I accepted and attended Makiki Christian Church for a few months. I met friends that were friendly and kind. I was impressed with the warmth and love displayed by these high school church friends and wanted what they had. That led to accept the invitation to attend the camp.

Pastor Paul Edwardson from Kapahulu Bible Church preached his final message on the last night. I cannot remember what he said. But its impact was powerful! At the close of his sermon, he invited the group to accept Christ into their lives. I remember stepping out into the aisle and walking forward with tears steaming down my face to accept this Jesus Christ. Hideo Kobayashi, a UH professor and youth worker, help lead me in a prayer to receive Jesus Christ into my heart as I wept my way into the kingdom of God.

I will never forget the scene that met me that night when I stepped outside the hall onto the balcony overlooking the Kaneohe Bay waters. The waters were still and peaceful as it reflected the lights from across the bay. I was magnetically drawn to that peaceful scenic bay waters and wondered why. And, then, I realized that the dynamic calm I was viewing was a reflection of the inner spiritual calm and peace I was experiencing for the first time in my life. Something deep within my heart had changed. I knew I would never be the same again.

That night I had found the God who created the stars I admired as a little child and had also found the answer to life after death. My search for the God of Creation and Eternity was over. I had found Him in Jesus Christ.

But I was only beginning to know Jesus. I was soon to discover Jesus as the One who wanted to baptize believers with the power of the Holy Spirit.

www.ingramcontent.com/pod-product-compliance
Lightning Source LLC
Chambersburg PA
CBHW021144020426
42331CB00005B/892